ORDERED STEPS

"How To Follow a Step by Step Christian Path To Get Closer With God"

Created, dedicated, and produced while engaged in new church planting work in the town of Spring Hill, Hernando County, Florida

www.facebook.com/PSHBC

We are the Redeemed living in the world for Jesus Christ redeeming one life at a time, expanding the Kingdom of God through preaching and teaching caretakers, children, and communities in crises.

Table of Contents

INTRODUCTION

Chapter

One   "... to the land I will show you." (Gen.12:1

Two   "...explore the land..." (Num 13:2)

Three "Break up your fallow ground," (Hosea 10:12)

Four   "The desolate land will be cultivated"
           (Ezekiel 26:24)

Five   "There is that scattereth, and yet increaseth..."
           (Prov. 11:24)

Six   "The seed is the word of God." (Luke 8:11)

Seven "What's important is that God makes the seed
           grow". (1Cor 3:7)

Eight "...and led them up a high mountain (top) by
           themselves." (Mark 9:2)

Concluding contribution by Rev. Dr. Loren J. Russell

"There are no shortcuts to any place worth going" Haynes Russell

INTRODUCTION

Using Michelle Alexander's book title: "The New Jim Crow, Mass Incarceration in a time of Color Blindness" and the Bible as a measuring rod, the following research was conducted and produced some food for thought.

The New York State Department of Corrections reports a prison population of approximately 53,662 inmates. The Florida Department of Corrections, however, operates the third largest state prison system in the United States. Its prison industrial complex is the largest agency in the State with a budget of $2.4 billion housing a little over 100,000 inmates incarcerated and another 115,000+ offenders under some type of community supervision.

The Florida Department of Corrections has 143 facilities statewide, including 43 major institutions, 33 work camps, 15 Annexes, 20 work release centers and 6 road prisons/forestry camps. It has more than 23,000 employees, about three-quarters of which are either certified correctional officers or probation officers.[1]

It is in the context of the above data and statistical lens the following devotional was produced to give God Glory and to edify, build up, and equip whosoever believes in Him, for the ministry and furtherance of the Gospel and for the sake of Jesus Christ.

---

[1]

http://en.wikipedia.org/wiki/Florida_Department_of_C orrections

The total area of Florida is 58,664 sq mi (151,939 sq km), of which land takes up 54,153 sq mi (140,256 sq km) and inland water 4,511 sq mi (11,683 sq km). Florida extends 361 mi (581 km) E–W; its maximum N–S extension is 447 mi (719 km). The state comprises a peninsula surrounded by ocean on three sides, with a panhandle of land in the NW. (State of Florida.com) Florida Geography Total Area - 58,560 Square Miles ... Florida's Population (2011) - 19,057,542 .

Ordered Steps is a compilation of step-by-step guide produced while planting Pristine Spring Hill Baptist Church with the help of members of the Nature Coast Baptist, and my friend pastor Omar Pablo from whom we received our first county permit for which to do ministry. At the beginning of each chapter are helpful one-line quotes submitted by Dr. H., an anonymous contributor. References are made remembering Newtown, Ferguson, and Staten Island New York. All photography was provided by Precious Memories, LLC., an affiliate of Pristine Baptist Church. Pristine Baptist Church and this writing was formed and compiled during a season of national, social, and political unrest. Between approximately October 2013 and December 2014, Pristine Baptist Church has ministered collectively to over 200 children belonging to families in crises in Spring Hill and Brooksville Florida who presently or formerly had at least one parent incarcerated. This publication was produced with the "least of these, my brethren…" in mind.

FOOD FOR THOUGHT!!!

Blessings

Rev. Dr. Emery L. Ailes, III

CHAPTER ONE

… to the land I will show you. (Gen.12:1)

God is able to do exceeding abundantly above all that we can ask of think. Dr. H

For the law of the Spirit of life in Christ Jesus hath made me free from the law of sin and death. (Rom. 8:2)

There is none holy as the Lord: for there is none beside thee: neither is there any rock like our God. (1 Samuel 2:2)

In spite of what it looks like, and what it feels like, and what it sounds like, and what it seems like, that if you are a child of the living God and a follower of the Lord Jesus Christ that you Worship the God Who makes all things possible even for what you are going through right now; for "Neither is there any

Rock Like our God!"

Live TO HELP SAVE someone who is in dire need.

Rejoice evermore. Pray without ceasing. In every thing give thanks: for this is the will of God in Christ Jesus concerning you. (1 Thess. 5:16-17)

In the text above we are encouraged to pray without ceasing. And that means that our lifestyle should be one of prayer. Pray about everything and worry about nothing. And the peace of God that surpasses all understanding shall keep you. Live Life on Purpose!!!!

Search me, O God, and know my heart: try me, and know my thoughts: And see if there be any wicked way in me, and lead me in the way everlasting. (Ps. 139:23)

The problem is some people don't want to be searched for fear of what they may find. King

David this in the text is asking to be searched and to be revealed by God. David faced real life challenges just as we do today. His answer to life's situations was to be searched. Our every waking desire ought to be for God's All Seeing Eye to do a personal fearless, moral and probing inventory of our hearts, minds, and souls.

For the word of the Lord is right; and all his works are done in truth. He loveth righteousness and judgment: the earth is full of the goodness of the Lord. (Ps 33.4)

Blessings beloved, in the very center of existence the Word of God reminds us Who the Owner of the earth really Is. The earth doesn't belong to the neither the most Red State nor the most Blue State. The earth does not belong to the country that owns the most guns, bombs, and gas. The Book Says that the earth is the Lord's. Not only is the earth His, but the fullness thereof; that means everything in it, and around it belongs to Him

Too. Therefore, the title of the message is:

Be Encouraged, God Is Greater

For therein is the righteousness of God revealed from faith to faith: as it is written, the just shall live by faith. (Rom 1.17)

Just Faith

Faith is all you need. You are even justified by your faith. Justification can mean just as if you did not sin. When the woman touched the hem of Jesus' garment, the Messiah Himself declared that it was her "faith" that had made her whole. So, what is faith? According to the above perspective, it is the main ingredient by which folk seeking Justice always live.

#gotfaith

Praise God praise God praise God. I humbly ask you to keep the prison ministry here in

Florida in your prayers. Here, the prison population is twice the amount populated in NY. The laws are older than Methuselah and more draconian than Hitler's Regime. The harvest is plenteous but the laborers are really few. Please pray that the Father send more laborers. It's Harvest Time!!!!

The Lord is not slack concerning his promise, as some men count slackness; but is longsuffering to us-ward, not willing that any should perish, but that all should come to repentance. (2 Pet 3:9)

Beloved, God is not Slack. He Will Do just what He Says He Will Do in His Timing, which is always perfect. Just because we can't see it, doesn't mean God cannot do it. In fact, God has Answered all of our prayers before we even ask or articulate them to Him. He's Is Sovereign and Always Working on you behalf.

We hope you have been blessed by the

biblical insights and inspiration in this chapter.

Rev. Dr. Emery L. Ailes, III, pastor

Pristine Spring Hill Baptist Church

Mailing: 14291 Spring Hill Dr Suite 118 Spring Hill Fl. 34609

352-515-4849

www.facebook.com/PSHBC

If you know of anyone in the Florida area that has family members incarcerated let us know. Visit us on facebook, call or inbox. Someone will be standing near waiting.

CHAPTER TWO

"…explore the land…" (Num 13:2)

Quality is not an accident. It is a habit. Dr. H

And we all, with unveiled face, beholding the glory of the Lord, are being transformed into the same image from one degree of glory to another. For this comes from the Lord who is the Spirit. (2 Cor. 2:18)

Today's scripture is interpreted for us in that we all are being changed daily. Transformation is constantly ever changing, yet at the same time remaining constant from one degree of glory to the next. In other words He is not through with you yet and there is more of you to be developed in Him.

It was during this season Pristine Spring Hill Baptist Church joined the Greater Hernando Chamber of Commerce.

CORRECTION: Our earlier post that was up on July 18 (4 p.m.) claiming that Eric Garner was apprehended by NYPD because Mr. Garner was breaking up a fight is incorrect and it is a statement out of context. Mr. Garner was being investigated over whether he was selling "loosies" or untaxed single cigarettes according to the NY Daily News.

"I can't breathe, I can't breathe", Eric Garner, 43, a married father of six children with two grandchildren, repeatedly screamed after at least five NYPD officers took him down in front of a Tompkinsville beauty supply store when he balked at being handcuffed.

Responsibility...

"Hold yourself responsible for a higher standard than anybody expects of you. Never excuse yourself."

— Henry Ward Beeche

Let all bitterness and wrath and anger and clamor and slander be put away from you, along with all malice. Be kind to one another, tenderhearted, forgiving one another, as God in Christ forgave you. (Ephesians 4:31)

For the eyes of the Lord are on the righteous, and his ears are open to their prayer. But the face of the Lord is against those who do evil." Now who is there to harm you if you are zealous for what is good? (1 Pet. 3.12)

Humble yourselves, therefore, under the mighty hand of God so that at the proper time he may exalt you,(1pet 5.6)

"We marched in solidarity with those in #Ferguson because we believed the people have a right to orderly and peaceful protest." Congressman John Lewis

When pride comes, then comes disgrace, but with the humble is wisdom. (Prov. 11:2)

Humble thyself, for if not life shall humble you.

God keeps those in perfect peace whose mind

is stayed on Him, because they trust in Him.

Do you not know that you are God's temple and that God's Spirit dwells in you?

Acts 4:31(NIV)

After they prayed, the place where they were meeting was shaken. And they were all filled with the Holy Spirit and spoke the word of God boldly.

Prayer changes things. From an early age, I witnessed this powerful truth through having a God fearing grandmother, Mrs. Tessie Ella Ailes, as one of my greatest earthy examples. She was among all a praying, God-fearing woman. Mommy, one morning, would be the first to have to articulate to a little baby 6 ½ year old boy that his daddy had died. And she taught me how to pray about it with her. And later, she'd always be sure to give God all glory when sharing the awesome news that

He had Comforted us all through those prayers. I remember and shall never forget.

Indeed, this is our confidence. Anything we pray for that aligns with the Father's Plan will be granted. And the more time we spend with Him, the more we'll come to understand His will and how to pray for it.

Remember, prayer doesn't change God's mind, but it does transform the believer's heart. Some requests are granted immediately, simply because we asked with the realization that our Father loves to give us good gifts. Other requests may require time or certain divine preparations before they can be given. We, meanwhile, must simply be diligent to persevere in prayer.

Whatever the Lord's response or timing, we trust that He has only the very best in store for His children. That means we might not receive exactly what we're asking for, but something even better. Such is God's great pleasure, for He alone perfectly knows each heart's desire and wishes to fulfill it.

Our most powerful tool for shaping the world and lives around us is always available. Prayer lets us witness God's hand in any situation. And as we give attention, time, and perseverance to conversation with Him, we find no limit to what He can achieve in people's hearts and circumstances.

We hope you have been blessed by the biblical insights and inspiration writing herein. Father, I pray that the content in this chapter succeeded in what Your Divine Plans are for the reader. Amen!!!

Rev. Dr. Emery Ailes, Senior Pastor

Pristine Baptist Church

CHAPTER THREE

Break up your fallow ground, (Hosea 10:12)

The task ahead of us is never as great as the Power behind us. Dr. H

Halleluiah,

Pastor Ailes has arrived at Pasco Hernando State College, Brooksville Campus in his new role as Professor of Humanities and Professional Tutor of English, Writing, and Speech.

God is So Great!!!!

Praise God of Heaven's Army!!!! His Name is Wonderful Counselor, King of Kings, Lord of Lords. Emanuel!!!!

Come to me, all who labor and are heavy laden, and I will give you rest. (Matt 11.28)

This is so simple. The problem in the world is the word "Independent." In our culture we celebrate Independence Day. Everyone wants to be "independent" and desire to "do it myself" and "I don't ask no one for anything" so much we disconnect and detach ourselves from commitments of all kinds. Children for the sake of independence de-commit from parents. Spouses de-commit from each other for the sake of individualism. People de-commit from the church, and become independent from God. Jesus says, "I am the true vine and ye the branches." It goes on to say that independent from Him we can do nothing.

The birds neither toil nor reap yet our heavenly Father feeds them. Aren't we more than birds?

The above verse makes it plain; depend on Him and His Word, not your own understanding. Just simply come to Him, and receive rest. Independence in this sense is sinful. Come unto me, Jesus says, and He Promises to give you rest, salvation, and a peace that surpasses all understanding.

He who dwells in the shelter of the Most High will abide in the shadow of the Almighty. I will say to the Lord, "My refuge and my fortress, my God, in whom I trust." (Ps. 91;1-2)

Surely He Shall hide thee and protect thee, and keep thee, and deliver thee!!!

I will sing praises, praises unto Him!!!

Listen to advice and accept instruction, that you may gain wisdom in the future. Many are the plans in the mind of a man, but it is the purpose of the Lord that will stand. (Prov. 19:20-21)

For thou hast possessed my reins: thou hast covered me in my mother's womb. I will praise thee; for I am fearfully and wonderfully made: marvelous are thy works; and that my soul knoweth right well. (Ps 139:13-14)

Enter into his gates with thanksgiving, and into his courts with praise: be thankful unto him, and bless his name. For the Lord is good; his mercy is everlasting; and his truth endureth to all generations. (Ps. 100:4-5)

This is the Day that The Lord has Made, let us rejoice and be glad in it!!!!

If you want an extra blessing on Sunday mornings you can meet pastor Ailes and the Pristine Spring Hill Baptist Church family at

10:00am at Beef O Brady's located on the corner of Spring Hill Drive and Barclay Ave in Spring Hill Florida where we will be lifting up the Name of Jesus.

It was during Domestic Violence Awareness season Pristine Spring Hill Baptist Church paused to observe October as Domestic Violence month.

Blessings

Beloved, we here at Pristine Spring Hill Baptist Church located in Hernando County are against Domestic Violence. Pray for us as we sit before and speak on behalf of God, through the lens of His Holy Word on this serious issue.

I have a serious concern to bring up with you, my friends, using the authority of Jesus, our Master. I'll put it as urgently as I can: You must get along with each other. You must learn to be considerate of one another, cultivating a life in common. (1 Cor. 1.10)

Let the healing process begin in His Name!!!!

Greetings Beloved,

I will praise you with an upright heart as I learn your righteous laws. (Ps. 119.7)

You are invited to Holy Communion every first Sunday at Pristine Spring Hill Baptist Church meeting inside Beef O'Brady's conference room at 10:30am where God and community meet. Come and get your blessing.

It was during the month of November 2014 the following was transcribed.

Every child has a story. For 2.7 million American children, that story is filled with the abandonment, loneliness and shame that come from having a mom or dad in prison. For many, it may also include following their parents down the same destructive road to incarceration.

That's why Pristine Spring Hill Baptist Church gives annual support to Angel Tree outreach programs.

Angel Tree, a program of Prison Fellowship, reaches out to the children of inmates and their families with the love of Christ. This unique program gives Pristine Spring Hill

Baptist Church of Hernando County an opportunity to share Christ's love by helping to meet the physical, emotional, and spiritual needs of the families of prisoners.

Matthew 25:36c "... I was in prison and you visited me"

Pray for us that God may be Glorified in our humble efforts to edify his people.

Neither is there salvation in any other: for there is no other name under heaven given among men, whereby we must be saved.

Jesus!!!!

Blessings Friends,

Days before The Messiah was to make the ultimate sacrifice for humankind; on retreat He uttered the following Words of Comfort while on retreat with his immediate Friends. This Jesus narrative can be found in the book of St. John chapter 14, starting at the 1st verse:

"Don't let your heart be troubled. Believe in

God. Believe also in me. - John 14:1

Today I want you to know that Jesus always loves to comfort you. He loves to put little candles in the darkened chambers of your sorrow. He loves to dry tears and change grief into joy. Then He is able to give comfort, because He has the comfort in Himself. We cannot give what we have not to give. We often say to one another in trial, "Do not worry! Do not be troubled!" When we have no comfort to give, nothing to cure the worry or brighten the darkness. Standing on the ship in the midst of a wild sea, Jesus said, "Peace!" and the winds and waves instantly became calm. He had the peace in Himself, and could give peace to the sea. When we have peace within, the same we can give to others. It is the same with Jesus' comfort: His words of consolation are not like so many of ours; they have power to quiet the troubled heart. When we have Jesus, we too have the power to comfort others.

It was a time of the deepest grief and the

sorest sorrow for the disciples when Jesus uttered the above verse. Not only were they to lose their best Friend, but they were to lose Him in the saddest way - by death in the shame of the cross. Nor was that all of their sorrow. They had hoped He was the Messiah; now that hope was gone. They were in utter desolation - in a starless midnight. Surely there could be no comfort for such grief as theirs, they thought that night, as with breaking hearts they sat there in the darkness.

Yet right into the midst of this despairing grief came the words, "Let not your heart be troubled." Let us never say, therefore, that there is any, even the bitterest, grief for which there is no possible comfort. No matter how dark the night is, Christ can put stars into our sky, and bring a glorious morning after the darkness. There is comfort for Christ's disciples in the most hopeless grief. We have but to look forward a few days to see the sorrow of these men turned to blessed joy. So it always is. However we may grieve, there is never any reason why we should lose our peace.

We hope you have been blessed by the biblical insights and inspiration in this chapter.

Rev. Dr. Emery L. Ailes, III, pastor

Pristine Spring Hill Baptist Church

352-515-4849

www.facebook.com/PSHBC

If you know of anyone in the Florida area that has family members incarcerated let us know. Visit us on facebook, call or inbox. Someone will be standing near waiting.

CHAPTER FOUR

"The desolate land will be cultivated" (Ezekiel 26:24)

Don't ask God to guide your footsteps unless you are willing to move. Dr. H

Blessings Friends,

Today's biblical principle is Be Encouraged. John the Beloved encouraging His Faithful believes, here, witnesses Jesus.

"These things I have spoken unto you, that in me ye might have peace. In the world ye shall have tribulation: but be of good cheer; I have overcome the world." (John 16:33)

His Words are just as encouraging today as they were to His Disciples. Peace, good cheer, and the transcendent ability to overcome belongs to you

The first job of leadership is to love people. Leadership without love is manipulation. Does your leadership have love? #love #leadership Theodore Roosevelt once remarked "Comparison is the Thief of joy." Do you have joy today?

Love finds us where we are not where we were. Has Love Found You?

#love

#God

Blessings Friends,

I have good news to share. with There is No Condemnation!!!!

Romans 8:1-2

Therefore there is now no condemnation for those who are in Christ Jesus. For the law of the Spirit of life in Christ Jesus has set you free from the law of sin and of death.

NO CONDEMNATION

Some believers are plagued by feelings of condemnation. Either they think they'll never live up to God's expectations for them or they're nearly drowning in guilt over past sins. These men and women cannot seem to shake the sense that God is displeased with their puny efforts at being Christ-like.

May I tell you something? The devil, my friends is a liar and the truth is not in him. The book of Romans confronts this lie head-on: "There is therefore no condemnation to those who are in Christ Jesus" (Rom. 8:1). When the Savior went to the cross on our behalf, He lifted the blame from our shoulders and made us righteous before God. Those feelings of condemnation do not belong to us; they are from Satan. He amplifies our guilt and feelings of inadequacy and then suggests that's how the Lord feels about His "wayward child." Nothing could be further from the truth. Our sins are wiped clean, and we are chosen and loved by God.

Condemnation is reserved for those who reject the Lord (John 3:36). Sin is a death sentence (Rom. 6:23). Anyone who chooses to cling to sin instead of seeking divine forgiveness must pay the penalty, which is an eternity separated from God. Two synonyms of condemn are 'denounce' and 'revile.' Those words certainly describe Jesus' statement to unbelievers in Matthew 25:41: "Depart from me, accursed ones."

There is no condemnation for those who receive Jesus Christ as their Savior. The believer's penalty for sin is paid, and he can stand blameless before God. Trust in the Lord's love and let go of Satan's lie. God's beloved children are covered by His grace and the sacrifice of Jesus Christ.

ALL our strength lies in PRAYER! Does yours?

Great Strength comes from Faith in God. Zech (12:5) Remembering all who fought, and that fight, and all who will fight for our country and their families.

Thine, O Lord, is the greatness, and the power, and the glory, and the victory, and the majesty: for all that is in the heaven and in the earth is thine; thine is the kingdom, O Lord, and thou art exalted as head above all. (1 Chron. 29:11)

In other words, to you, O God, belong the greatness and the might, the glory, the victory, the majesty, the splendor; Yes! Everything in heaven, everything on earth; the kingdom all yours! You've raised yourself high over all. Riches and glory come from you, you're ruler over all; You hold strength and power in the palm of your hand to build up and strengthen all. And here we are, O God, our God, giving thanks to you, praising your Name!!!

God's plan for your life exceeds circumstances of a bad week.

Pristine Spring Hill Baptist Church, where God and community meet.

Greetings Friends,

In the nearness of Advent Pristine Spring Hill Baptist Church we would like to encourage all to start where you are. Use what you have. Do what you can for the greater God, which is in Christ Jesus!!!!

Oswald Chambers explains what faith is. "Faith is the deliberate confidence in the character of God whose ways you may not understand at the time."

Racism is a SIN problem, not a SKIN problem!

Racism is an expression of narcissism.

'Anyone says 'I love God' but hates others is a liar." 1 John 4:20

"Anyone who does not love the people that we CAN see, CANNOT love God whom we do not see!" 1 John 4:20

"If you are nice only to your people, you are no better than everyone else. Even unbelievers do that!" -JESUS , Matthew 5:47

"Whoever hates others is walking around in darkness... and is completely blinded." 1 John 2:11

"Anyone who hates his brother is a murderer, and no murderer has eternal life in him!" 1 John 3:15

"I tell you this clearly: You must love even your enemies and you must do good even to those who hate you."- JESUS Luke 6:27

Racism is an insult to your Creator. GOD chose to make each person the race he wanted them to be, including you.

We hope you have been blessed by the biblical insights and inspiration writing herein. Father, I pray that the content in this chapter succeeded in what Your Divine Plans are for the reader. Amen!!!

Rev. Dr. Emery Ailes, Senior Pastor

Pristine Baptist Church

CHAPTER FIVE

"There is that scattereth, and yet increaseth…" (Prov. 11:24)

Honor is the Ladder upon which all virtues ascend. Dr. H

The Name

Philippians 2:9-10

Wherefore God also hath highly exalted him, and given him a name which is above every name: **That at the name of Jesus** every knee should bow, of things in heaven, and things in earth, and things under the earth; (Philippians 2:9-10 KJV)

The Bible ascribes many different **names to Jesus**, all of which provide great insight into His character and person. Here are some from John's gospel that I find particularly revealing:

The Good Shepherd (10:11) protects his sheep at all cost from predators. They know His voice and follow Him.

The Door (vv. 7-9) is the only way to enter heaven. Whoever enters through the "gate" of Christ will be saved.

The Vine (15:1-10) is the source of our spiritual life. When we stay intimately connected to Jesus, we bear fruit. If we do not remain in Him, we wither.

The Bread of Life (6:25-35) the only one who can truly satisfy our hearts. Jesus feeds our souls with sustenance that never leaves us wanting for more.

The Light of the World (9:5) shines His light through our countenance as a ministry and testimony to a dark world.

The Way **(14:6) to happiness, peace, joy, and eternal life is Jesus Christ.**

The Truth (14:6) of His revelation, as recorded in the New Testament, is the reason we can know as much as we do about God.

The Life (14:6) Jesus imparts to believers is powerful, effective, and fruitful, not only in eternity but here on earth as well.

In biblical times, Israelites would choose a baby's name based on the child's characteristics or a hope or prayer of the parent. The names given to Jesus tell a great deal about His ministry on earth 2,000 years ago. The scriptural names describing Him reveal who He was and is and will be for eternity.

Greetings Beloved,

With the Advent of our Lord and Savior's Birth, Let's for a moment talk about a favorite pastime for many this Christmas Season....Spending Money.

Spending Our Inheritance Wisely

Ephesians 1: 11 also we have obtained an inheritance, having been predestined according to His purpose who works all things after the counsel of His will.

Spending Our Inheritance Wisely

The word "inheritance" usually brings to mind the money and real estate handed down from one generation to another. But God has an even greater legacy to share with His children—one that they are given the moment they enter His family.

Galatians 4:7 tells us that believers are God's heirs. First among our priceless treasures is a living hope in Jesus Christ that cannot be taken away (1 Peter 1:3). What's more, He pledged to supply our needs according to His riches (Phil 4:19). In other words, we already have all that we need for an abundant and victorious life.

However, some folks get stuck in spiritual poverty because they refuse to view themselves as adopted children. Failing to tap into their inheritance, they're like a man who sees himself as a poor, sinful creature: he wanders through this big angry world hoping to hold on to his meager scrap of faith until he's lucky enough to die and go to heaven. Of course that man misses the blessings available in this life, because he's not looking for them.

How differently people see themselves when they look through the eyes of Jesus. Christians who live like the beloved, empowered heirs that they are will lavishly spend their inheritance of grace to benefit everyone they meet.

God gives all believers a pledge of inheritance out of the unsurpassed riches of His infinite grace. We are spiritually rich citizens of heaven who have nothing to fear in this world. Choose to live boldly for Christ, and see how abundantly God pours out blessing from the legacy already set aside for you.

Two years later, it's a tragedy that still hurts our hearts as we all hope for healing. #RememberNewtown

Be joyful always; pray continually, give thanks in all circumstances –1 Thess 5:16-18

Our Prince of Peace

Isaiah 9:6

The Christmas rush is here. There are plans to make, gifts to buy, and parties to attend. Sometimes these activities leave us exhausted and cranky—instead of peace and joy, we may feel inner churning because there's too much to do. Or perhaps this time of the year brings nothing but sad memories and loneliness. Unrealistic expectations and conflicts with loved ones often leave us depressed and discouraged.

How can Jesus be our Prince of Peace when our expectations and traditions fight against the tranquility we desire? To understand why Jesus was given this title, we must first understand what it means. First of all, God's Son did not come to do away with all conflicts—not yet, anyway. One day He will return to earth and rule as King in an environment of external harmony, but that was not the purpose of His first coming. So while we're on earth, we'll have trouble (John 16:33).

When Christ left heaven to become a human baby, His goal was to bring us peace with God by reconciling us to the Father. His death on the cross paid our sin debt in full, and our relationship with God is restored. Now He offers us divine peace—an inner serenity that fills our hearts and minds no matter what is going on in our circumstances.

Is your life characterized by a quiet assurance that guards your heart and mind all day long (Phil. 4:6-7), or have stressful circumstances left you feeling depressed or agitated? Try setting aside time each day to fix your eyes upon Jesus. Then let Him heal your heart and calm your spirit.

I know who goes before me. I know who stands behind. The God of angel armies is always by my side. ~Whom Shall I Fear

Antioch Fellowship Missionary Baptist, Chic-fil-A, Prison Fellowship and Pastor Pristine Baptist co-sponsored Angel Tree Celebration with invited guest.

To God Be The Glory!!!!

And though I have the gift of prophecy, and understand all mysteries, and all knowledge; and though I have all faith, so that I could remove mountains, and have not LOVE, I am nothing. (1 Cor. 13:2)

Love is the one principle that will last you a lifetime and make you a conqueror over all things. Love covers a multitude of sin and is the key to life. Hug somebody and tell them you love them. It may be the only time someone says something nice to a person. You will discover its contagion, meaning if you love someone, then they'll love another. They may even love you back!!!!

Courageous people have decided they're not living afraid anymore. - Bob Goff

We hope you have been blessed by the biblical insights and inspiration in this chapter.

Rev. Dr. Emery L. Ailes, III, pastor
Pristine Spring Hill Baptist Church
352-515-4849
www.facebook.com/PSHBC

If you know of anyone in the Florida area that has family members incarcerated let us know. Visit us on facebook, call or inbox. Someone will be standing near waiting.

CHAPTER SIX

"The seed is the word of God." (Luke 8:11)
In everything give thanks. Dr. H

My morning God Song is: I will sing aloud of thy mercy in the morning: for thou hast been my defense and refuge in the day of my trouble. Psalm 59:16

Blessings Beloved,

Setting Goals for Fruitful Living

2 Samuel 7:18

" Then David the king went in and sat before the LORD, and he said, "Who am I, O Lord GOD, and what is my house, that You have brought me this far?"

Some time ago, I experienced a turning point in my ministry as a spiritual counselor walking with Christ thereby developing a system I use to help enhance individuals mature spiritually for life.

It started with 2 Samuel 7, which inspired me to follow in King David's footsteps. He spent time alone with God, offering praise and thanksgiving. He would also listen as the Lord revealed truth and offered insight about the future. Because of what he learned, David was able to set goals and stay aligned with them.

Desiring that kind of solitude from 2003-2012, I spent several years alone in seminary at Alliance Theological seminary and Theological School at Drew University, respectively. Most of the time, I was silent, listening intently for God's voice. I asked Him to speak to me regarding my future, and He answered. Using a journal, I recorded the goals He inspired. The things He communicated so impacted my choices and so greatly blessed me that I continued the discipline even today at the rewriting of today's inspiration.

Let's discuss how to establish aims in this manner. First, come before the throne of Almighty God with a repentant heart, praise, and thanksgiving. Then, ask Him for direction in areas such as spiritual life, career, and family. In silence, wait patiently and attentively—as you read and meditate upon God's Word, He will speak. Most often, His guidance is experienced as a prodding or conviction in the heart. When that happens, be sure to write down what you're "hearing" so you can review it later.

In order to stay on the path God intends for our lives, we should plan times to stop, ask, and listen for guidance. The world throws confusing messages at us all day long, and we need to check our course frequently. These conversations with the Lord are vital for a thriving life of godly impact.

Blessings Friends,

In today's meditation speaking to us through the Oracle of Psalms, God wants us to be secure in knowing that He Is our Trustworthy Guide throughout life and eternity.

TRUSTWORTHY IS our GUIDE

Ps. 32:8-9 I will instruct you and teach you in the way which you should go; I will counsel you with My eye upon you. Do not be as the horse or as the mule which have no understanding, Whose trappings include bit and bridle to hold them in check, Otherwise they will not come near to you.

TRUSTWORTHY IS our GUIDE

There is a well-known picture that exists that shows the Lord Jesus standing behind a young man whose eyes are focused in the direction that the Master is pointing. Jesus' hand is on the man's shoulder, and I imagine He is saying, "This is the way we're going. I will get you to the destination." Although the road will be marked with both joy and suffering, the Lord leads His followers all the way to their eternal home.

Anyone who is honest will admit that he or she is ill-equipped to go through life alone. Our all-knowing God created us with a need for His guidance. In our own strength, knowledge, and reasoning power, we are simply not able to figure out how to make the wisest decisions. But the Lord's assuring hand at our shoulder can lead us down right paths to good choices.

The Lord is willing and able to guide us, if we will let Him. It isn't difficult to fall in step with Him. Acknowledge that you have wandered down paths of life that led to sin and disobedience. Choose to follow His lead instead by reading the Word of God and applying biblical principles to your life. And learn to pray through both large and small decisions as you seek the path He has set for you.

While visiting a friend Deacon Blues over the holidays I was enlightened by the Spirit of God. Perhaps we don't talk about it much because somehow we feel earth is our final destination. But as we age and look back at our lives we realize that just beyond our last heartbeat lies eternity. That's where our Savior is pointing us. The path may not be clear to our eyes, but Jesus is leading us there with a steady and sure hand. Our part is to follow in obedience so that we may reach heaven and hear the Father say, "Well done."

Keep the faith!!!

.....and just in case you did not know, in spite of all that you have had to endure, you were made to be Victorious!!!! Amen

Blessings Beloved,

The saints of the Living God are under attack and heavily engaged in spiritual warfare. The God of peace will soon crush Satan under your feet. Romans 16:20

Just in case there is someone in fear that they have sinned beyond repair, we want you to know today that God Is Our Loving Father.

Luke 15:19-20

I am no longer worthy to be called your son; make me as one of your hired men."' 20 "So he got up and came to his father. But while he was still a long way off, his father saw him and felt compassion for him, and ran and embraced him and kissed him.

Humanity tends to project its own faulty habits onto God. This is especially true regarding the nature of His love. We think we must barter, plead, or try hard to earn the Lord's favor. But as the prodigal son learned, the Father's love is unconditional.

The wayward son expected his father's love to be diminished. Therefore, he went home hoping for a place among the family servants. Imagine the boy's delight when Dad greeted him with a hug and a celebration. His actions certainly didn't merit an outpouring of affection, but Jesus' parable is all about a Father who doesn't give people what they deserve.

A love based on conduct would keep people guessing, have I done enough? Instead, God cares for you simply because you're you, and He expects nothing in return. Consider the prodigal's life after his homecoming party. He didn't move into the servants' quarters and get to work. He was reinstated to his place as the second son of a wealthy man, with all of the privilege that entails. In the same way, believers are the Lord's cherished children (2 Cor. 6:18). When God looks at His loved ones, He doesn't focus upon past failures, faults, or sin. He sees the heirs to His kingdom—men and women who love Him and desire to spend eternity in His presence.

No matter how far we may wander from the

Lord's perfect will for our lives, we are always welcome back. The Bible teaches that God's love cannot be lost, regardless of sin or poor decisions (though we may have to live with the consequences). Our Father's arms are always open.

May God Bless you and Heal and draw you nearer everyday.

Jesus Come make my heart Your Home

We hope you have been blessed by the biblical insights and inspiration in this chapter.

We hope you have been blessed by the biblical insights and inspiration writing herein. Father, I pray that the content in this chapter succeeded in what Your Divine Plans are for the reader. Amen!!!

Rev. Dr. Emery Ailes, Senior Pastor

Pristine Baptist Church

CHAPTER SEVEN

"What's important is that God makes the seed grow". (1Cor 3:7)

If you only do what you know you can do you will never do very much. Dr. H

In answering the question of Godliness, Jesus says...

"But go and learn what this means: 'I DESIRE COMPASSION, AND NOT SACRIFICE,' for I did not come to call the righteous, but sinners." (Matthew 9:13)

Answer to the question of Godliness!!

There is a common misconception that believers should be perfect. Pretending to have our lives in order, many of us wear happy faces and speak words that sound acceptable. At times we're ashamed to admit our shortcomings, as if they should not exist. Salvation through Jesus, however, doesn't change the fact that sin is present in our life. If you do not remember anything from today's inspiration, please remember and retain the following: When we're born again, God forgives us and sees us as righteous!!!! Yet our battle with sin continues till we arrive in heaven.

It's not about achieving perfection in and of itself. In fact, in a great sense, striving for perfection actually can be a trap that pulls us away from living a godly life. Functioning in this way is a form of relying on our own capability. Jesus said that He came to heal the spiritually sick because they recognized their weakness. With an awareness of our inadequacy comes the realization of our need for Him.

The world sees successful individuals as powerful and self-sufficient, but Jesus didn't care about these qualities. Instead, He wants people to be aware of their own brokenness. This is the foundation for godliness. Conversely, drawing from a 12 step program principle, the first step is to admit one's powerlessness.

We should accept our neediness and seek God passionately. Doing so allows the following attributes to develop: a hunger for

God's Word, faithful service, deepening trust, and decision-making based upon principle rather than preference. Patiently and mercifully, God matures us.

Be careful not to cover up your sins in order to look like a "good Christian." Without recognition and confession of our sinfulness, we are unable to rely fully on God. It is only with this awareness that we can passionately seek Him, obey in His strength, and confess with repentance when we miss the mark.

Blessings Beloved,

Throughout life you meet people who are not God Conscious for various reasons. Therefore, this inspiration is fitly titled

Godly Living in an Ungodly Age...what do you do with that?

"For the overseer must be above reproach as God's steward, not self-willed, not quick-tempered, not addicted to wine, not pugnacious, not fond of sordid gain, but hospitable, loving what is good, sensible, just, devout, self-controlled." (Titus 1 7-8)

Godly Living in an Ungodly Age...as Christians what do we do with that?

Our Founding Fathers of American western culture created a governing framework based upon biblical principles. Slowly, we have changed from "one nation under God" to a group of people who no longer want Him to be involved.

Tragically, we've become, in numerous ways, an ungodly nation: many are driven by materialism and power; immorality and rebellion are prevalent; empty philosophy and false doctrine are widely acceptable. Underlying it all is a vocal decision to take God out of the nation's "official business." Take prayer out of schools; even groups that claim to have schools and youth groups in their best interests.

Yet even in an unbelieving society, people can, as individuals, follow Jesus. But the world will continually disseminate faulty teachings, so believers must be discerning. Otherwise, erroneous messages and peer pressure can lead Christians to compromise their convictions. Then affections and priorities may change. Don't let the world's clamor make the Spirit's voice less audible. Without His guidance, our minds become vulnerable to lies.

The Word of God is a compass that keeps us headed in the right direction—even in the midst of confusing messages all around. We need to be consistently filled with truth by reading, believing, meditating upon, and applying Scripture. God is Clear from New York, to Florida, to San Francisco; He instructs us to "pray without ceasing" (1 Thess. 5:17). If our minds are focused upon Him, unholy beliefs will not be able to take root.

The Word is our guidebook. We will still face difficulty as we live in this imperfect world—it is a confusing, dark place that entices us but never fulfills our true longings. Yet God's truth will bring confidence and boldness, and His Spirit will direct and strengthen, enabling us to live victoriously.

God Appointed Angels Watching Over us!!!!!

Keep watch because the devil is on the prowl.

He gave Himself to be slain...Will you trust HIM?

Though he slay me, yet will I trust in him Job 13:15

~10 WAYS TO LOVE~

Listen
without interrupting

Share
without pretending

Speak
without accusing

Enjoy
without complaint

Give
without sparing

Trust
without wavering

Pray
without ceasing

Forgive
without punishing

Answer
without arguing

Promise
without forgetting

But thou O Lord art a shield for me; my glory, and the lifter up of my head. Psalm 3:3

…the joy of the LORD is your strength. Nehemiah 8:10

This is the day that the Lord has made. Let Us Rejoice and be glad in it.

I was glad when they said unto me "Let us go unto the house of the Lord!!!!"

A man of many companions may be ruined, but there is a friend who sticks closer than a brother. (Prov. 18:24)

We hope you have been blessed by the biblical insights and inspiration in this chapter.

We hope you have been blessed by the biblical insights and inspiration writing herein. Father, I pray that the content in this chapter succeeded in what Your Divine Plans are for the reader. Amen!!!

Rev. Dr. Emery Ailes, Senior Pastor
Pristine Baptist Church

CHAPTER EIGHT

"...and led them up a high mountain (top) by themselves." (Mark 9:2)

A new year means new responsibilities, new opportunities, and new mercies. Dr. H

As we commemorate today the life and legacy of Rev. Dr. Martin Luther King Jr., let's remember to whom he (and we all) ultimately report.

Use me, God. Show me how to take who I am, who I want to be, and what I can do, and use it for a purpose greater than myself. – Martin Luther King Jr.

Blessings Beloved and Happy Martin Luther King Jr. day 2015.

Romans 14:22 The faith which you have, have as your own conviction before God. Happy is he who does not condemn him self in what he approves.

Convictions Over Conveniences

Today, the nation pauses; the banks are closed as we celebrate the life and legacy of one of God's servant the Rev. Dr. Martin Luther King Jr., whose monument stands in our nations Capitol overlooking the Potomac River. His godly convictions compelled and gripped him to love all people because "hate is too great of a burden to bear."

A person of conviction has become convinced, by either evidence or argument, that his beliefs are true. Today, most men and women would rather live by preference than conviction. They choose to believe something based on certain conditions and circumstances. When the situation changes, so does their loyalty. In other words, a lot of people vacillate on issues that require a firm resolve.

Contrast this wishy-washy approach with the mindset of the great men and women of Scripture. Despite many years of unfair treatment, Joseph never wavered in his commitment to godly principles. As a result, he was in the right place at the right time to ensure Israel's survival (Gen. 50:20). Daniel, another righteous man in an idolatrous land, earned the trust of foreign kings by standing firm in his beliefs (Dan. 1:20). When his friends Shadrach, Meshach, and Abednego also refused to compromise their beliefs, they influenced a king to recognize Jehovah as the one true God (3:29).

As these biblical heroes show, godly convictions can withstand the changing winds of opinion and the persuasive arguments of opponents. If we are grounded in the Word and trust what God has said, we can stand firm in our beliefs. Confidence breeds the courage to remain strong amid conflict.

Instead of following your own preferences, choose to live by godly conviction. The Bible has much to say about the most important aspects of your life. See if God's principles and promises hold true. Through prayer and study, allow Him to firmly root you in solid biblical convictions.

Though you have not seen him, you love him; and even though you do not see him now, you believe in him and are filled with an inexpressible and glorious joy. 1 Peter 1:8-9

May the God of hope fill you with all joy and peace, as you trust in Him. Romans 15:13

Think about it, someone had to hurt so that we can heal; even die so that we can live.

...And by his stripes we are healed. Isaiah 53:5

The BODY of Christ a.k.a. The CHURCH

So, Do We Really Need One Another?

1 Corinthians 12:12

12 For even as the body is one and yet has many members, and all the members of the body, though they are many, are one body, so also in Christ.

Why bother or concern ourselves or associate ourselves with others? Has coming together for worship and sharing as one become obsolete and over rated? Is it at all necessary? Do we really need one another, or is the alternative truer?

Believers have two responsibilities. The first is to worship God and the second is to work for His kingdom. Where and how we serve is based upon our unique talents, skills, and callings. But the one place where we are all expected to give of ourselves is the local church.

When you were saved, the Lord baptized you by the Holy Spirit into His church—the body of believers who live all over the world but are united by trust in Jesus Christ. You then chose, according to the will of God, to become part of a local, autonomous group of believers. He placed you there because He knows that you are needed (1 Cor. 12:18). You are significant to your home church.

The church is more than a community. It is an interdependent body with individual members who were created by God to function in communion with one another. We Christians, like the world at large, are a diverse group, and that means we often have to strive hard for unity. But our differences are actually something to be celebrated, because each person uniquely contributes to God's purpose. A church that is truly operating as a unit—with all its varied gifts, talents, personalities, and intellects focused toward kingdom goals—must be a beautiful sight before the Lord.

Christianity isn't a spectator religion. We all have jobs to do in God's kingdom. The body of Christ functions best and most beautifully when all members resolve to serve God and each other to the best of their ability (v. 25). What are you doing for your church?

Pristine Spring Hill Baptist Church
Rev. Dr. Ailes, Senior Pastor
Worship Sundays @ Conference Room Beef
O' Brady's 10:30am
14387 Spring Hill Drive Spring Hill FL 34609
Come and be blessed!!!!

We are the Redeemed living on earth for Jesus Christ; redeeming the times one life at a time, expanding the Kingdom of God through preaching and teaching caretakers, children, and communities in crises.

In contributory conclusion,

THE BENEFIT OF LOVING RELATIONSHIPS

Recently, a friend posted on Facebook a dilemma he was facing that was challenging his relationship with the young lady he had chosen to develop a serious relationship with. In part, it seems that he felt emotionally, financially, and personally he was not getting in return the same measure that he was giving. How sad to think that anyone would opt to discontinue giving because they aren't getting the same in return.

That's one of the tragedies of modern day romances, i.e., the expectation of mutual and immediate reciprocity. Somehow, we have gotten the impression that our significant others are bound to give back to us in the same proportion and at the same way that we give. Many times we expect even more. However, that way of thinking is antithetical, detrimental, and has no biblical foundation.

There are many scriptures that seemingly point to mutual and immediate reciprocity as a reward for doing good or for giving to others, especially our significant others. Some would seek to justify that notion by pointing to Matthew 7:12, "In everything, do to others what you would have them do to you, for this sums up the law and the Prophets" (NIV). The problem with using the "Golden Rule" as a reference (as it is for so many scriptures that seemingly give credence to the idea of mutual reciprocity) is that it never indicates a reciprocity because of your *doing* or *giving*. It says "'*do*' to others what you *would have* them '*do*' unto you." The implication here is that when you '*do*', be not in expectation of getting something in return. Simply '*do*' because you have it in you to '*do*' and because it's the right thing to '*do*.' '*Do*' in contemplation of receiving equal back, and whatever you get back *is* your reward. All long term, down the road, long-lasting benefits are forfeited for the sake of immediate and proportionate reciprocity.

Some would point to Luke 6:38, "Give, and it shall be given unto you; good measure, pressed down, and shaken together, and running over, shall men give into your bosom. For with the same measure that ye mete withal it shall be measured to you again" (KJV). Again, the challenge is in the interpretation. This scripture does in fact say you will have proportional reciprocation, but it does not promise immediate reciprocity. And nowhere does it say it will be in the *form* or the *way* you want it.

My direct response to my friend was pretty straight forward; "What I have learned in my 28 years of marriage is that I give because I have it to give. Giving completes *me*! My reward is in my giving. What doesn't come back is not needed. Sometimes what comes back is what I *need*, not what I want, so it's easily missed or misunderstood. So don't let what someone isn't capable of giving to you stop you from giving to them what you have to give."

Be Blessed!

Rev. Dr. J. Loren Russell, BS, M.Div. D.Min.

www.ingramcontent.com/pod-product-compliance
Lightning Source LLC
Chambersburg PA
CBHW040035110426
42741CB00031B/108